AWARD CRITERIA

Fourteenth Edition

Mark Graham Brown

CRC Press
Taylor & Francis Group
Boca Raton London New York

CRC Press is an imprint of the
Taylor & Francis Group, an **informa** business

A PRODUCTIVITY PRESS BOOK

Productivity Press
Taylor & Francis Group
270 Madison Avenue
New York, NY 10016

Visit the Taylor & Francis Web site at
http://www.taylorandfrancis.com

and the Productivity Press Web site at
http://www.productivitypress.com

Table of Contents

Acknowledgments

I would like to thank the following individuals for their suggestions to improve the first edition of this book: Carol Pletcher, Cargill; Martin Smith, New England Telephone; Ann Wolfe, Air Products and Chemicals; Craig Skrivseth, Appleton Papers. I also wish to thank Jim Springer of Appleton Papers, who gave me the idea for this book, and Lynn Berner-Kilbourn who did an exceptional job of editing and formatting the original book.

I would also like to thank Michael Sinocchi, senior acquisitions editor at Productivity Press, for his outstanding editing over the years.

—MGB

Introduction

This guide is designed to help you understand the criteria for the Malcolm Baldrige National Quality Award. It is not about the award, or how to win it. Rather, it is about how to interpret and use the criteria to improve your organization.

Most organizations that use the Baldrige criteria have no interest in applying for, or winning, the award. The Baldrige criteria are being used by thousands of organizations around the world to evaluate their progress toward becoming the best in their fields. This guide is divided into two parts. Part. I, a question and answer section, provides the answers to the questions most commonly asked about the award and the criteria. Part II provides a brief explanation of each of the 18 items in the Baldrige criteria and lists the characteristics of organizations that excel in each of these 18 items.

If the material in this quick reference guide sparks your interest in the Baldrige criteria or the Malcolm Baldrige National Quality Award, you can obtain more information from the sources listed at the end of the book.

P A R T I
QUESTIONS &
ANSWERS

Answers to some of the questions frequently asked about the Malcolm Baldrige National Quality Award criteria.

Q: Why is our organization using the Baldrige criteria to do assessments?

A: Since the award was first established in 1988, there have been thousands of organizations that have applied for the award. Thousands more have applied for state quality awards, and several million copies of the criteria have been distributed to organizations all over the world. Many organizations have no interest in applying for the award, but use the criteria as a model for evaluating and improving their own performance. The criteria in the Baldrige model are the toughest and most widely accepted set of standards for defining a well run organization, regardless of its size or type.

The real rewards for following the Baldrige model are:
- More satisfied customers and stakeholders.
- Engaged employees.
- Improved financial results and outcomes.
- Long-term success.

Q: How does the Baldrige model fit with other improvement initiatives like CRM (customer relationship management), Joint Commission, Six Sigma, Balanced Scorecard, Knowledge Management, and Lean?

A: The Baldrige criteria are much more comprehensive than any of the programs or initiatives listed above. Further, the Baldrige model does not require that you follow or use any of these initiatives. Baldrige should be thought of as a "nondenominational" model that does not require you to follow any program or management guru. However, you will find that efforts made to implement any of programs or initiatives listed above will help you on your quest to deploy the Baldrige model. The core values and criteria used to assess organizations in the Baldrige model are consistent with those found in the programs listed above. If you find that the programs above are working for you—great! If you are not doing any of these things, you may also end up with high scores on a Baldrige assessment by developing your own approaches to managing customers, measurements, and work processes.

Q: What are the benefits of following the Baldrige model?

A: There are many benefits and financial reasons for adopting this model. Baldrige winners that are publicly traded companies have outperformed the Standard & Poor's Index by up to 6 times in 10 of the last 13 years. Even companies that are good enough to be Baldrige finalists have outperformed the index by 2 to 1. It is hard to ignore data that clearly indicates that adopting the Baldrige criteria greatly increases the chance of market success. If you are a school, hospital, or other nonprofit organization, or a privately owned firm, there are still many benefits. In addition to improved financial management and performance, organizations that score high on Baldrige reveal much higher employee satisfaction and have happy and loyal customers and stakeholders. These organizations also tend to be successful over long periods of time and are among the best in their respective fields.

Q: Do we have to go through the actual award application process to find out how we stack up against the criteria?

A: Certainly not. There are many ways of finding out how you perform against the criteria without writing the full 50-page application and applying for the award. Most states have their own Baldrige-based awards that offer condensed applications, often less than 15 pages. There is also a brief questionnaire developed by the government called Are We Making Progress? You may download this survey at no charge from the Baldrige website, www.quality.nist.gov. Some organizations perform focus group assessments, listing strengths and areas for improvement for each of the Baldrige items. For additional information on Baldrige assessment approaches, consult my larger text: Baldrige Award Winning Quality, available from Productivity Press (see inside back cover of this book).

Q: How do I apply the Baldrige criteria to assess a facility or department?

A: The criteria are written to assess an entire company or a single business unit. To use the Baldrige criteria to evaluate your facility or department, you need to translate slightly. It is helpful to look at your department or facility as a separate company. Imagine that everyone in your department left the company and formed an organization that sells your services back to the company. From this perspective it is easier to determine who your customers are, and what products/services you provide for them.

In the Baldrige criteria, the word "customer" refers to external customers. Because all of your customers may be inside the company, you need to apply a broader meaning to words like "customer" and "supplier."

Similarly, when assessing areas such as human resources or corporate citizenship, put the item in the context of your department or facility.

Q: What are the seven categories in the Baldrige criteria, and what do they focus on?

A: The seven categories in the Baldrige criteria and their corresponding point values are as follows:

1. Leadership   120 points
2. Strategic Planning   85 points

3. Customer and Market Focus   85 points
4. Measurement, Analysis, and
   Knowledge Management   90 points
5. Workforce Focus   85 points
6. Process Management   85 points
7. Results   450 points

TOTAL 1,000 points

Fifty-five percent of the points in the Baldrige criteria focus on how the organization is run; the remaining 45 percent of the points focus on the results achieved. Categories 1 through 6 (550 points) focus on the company's approaches or systems.

The criteria do not tell you the best method for running your business. Rather, they look for evidence of a systematic approach that is tailored to the needs of your business and culture. Category 7, Results, asks about your financial, customer, and employee satisfaction performance. All important results in running a business are assessed.

The seven categories of the Baldrige criteria are subdivided into 18 items, which are further subdivided into the 32 areas that must be addressed. The figure below shows how the criteria are organized. This guide explains each of the

18 examination items. The 32 areas to address are not covered in detail.

The Baldrige Criteria

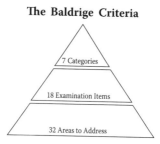

7 Categories

18 Examination Items

32 Areas to Address

Q: How do the seven categories work together as a system?

A: By definition, a system is a series of processes that are followed sequentially to achieve a desired result. Each of the major components of the system has inputs, processes, outputs of results, and, ideally, feedback loops. The figure on the inside front cover shows how the Baldrige criteria work as a system.

In the Baldrige criteria as a system, the learning of customers' wants and needs are the inputs (Item 3.1). On the basis of that input, the leadership sets the direction of the company, and defines its mission, values, products and/or services (Category 1: Leadership).

Next, the company decides on its overall strategy for success, identifies performance metrics, and sets goals for improvement (Category 2: Strategic Planning and Category 4: Measurement, Analysis, and Knowledge Management).

Once measures and plans have been developed, the company designs systems and processes for its people (Category 5: Workforce Focus) and its customers (3.2 Customer Relationships and Satisfaction), and its major work processes (Category 6: Process Management).

All of these systems should produce internal results such as sales, profits, and high quality products and services, and external results such as customer satisfaction and repeat business or market share (Category 7: Results).

Every item in the Baldrige criteria that asks about approaches and the implementation of approaches also asks about built-in feedback loops and continuous improvement.

Q: How are the 2008 Baldrige criteria different from previous years?

A: The criteria did not change from 2007 to 2008. A fairly substantial rewrite was performed in 2007, so this year required little alteration. This biannual overhaul schedule has been the pattern or many years as the criteria become more mature. One area that did change is the scoring scale for results. Since results are worth 45% of the points, this is worth some attention. The new scoring scale for results still ranges from 0% to 100%, but the scoring bands include more specifics on scoring four different dimensions of performance results: Levels, Trends, Comparisons, and Integration. A new acronym has been created for the four dimensions—LeTCI ("let's see")—suggesting that the examiners want to "see" how well the organization is performing.

Q: Can you explain how the Baldrige criteria create a roadmap for a better organization?

A: The Baldrige criteria have become the world's most widely accepted model for running an effective organization. The criteria cover almost everything that impacts on running a successful organization. The best way to understand this is to list some very basic factors a successful organization must consider, and to identify where these factors are addressed in the Baldrige criteria. Table 1 provides a list of activities successful companies typically perform, along with the Baldrige criteria item that corresponds to the activity.

Q: How do the Baldrige criteria apply to a small organization?

A: The items in the criteria are relevant to a small business as well as a big corporation. Small businesses must have good systems and results to keep them in business. The basic difference in your approach as a small organization is the level of formality. A small organization does not necessarily need a formal strategic plan or product development and supplier management system. It does need at least an informal approach to all of the elements in the Baldrige criteria, however. For example, you might not need a structured training curriculum for new employees if you only have 25 of them. You might use structured on-the-job training, however, as a way of bringing new hires

Table 1: The Baldrige Criteria — A Roadmap for Success

What Successful Organizations Do	Corresponding Baldrige Items
■ Identify and segment customers/stakeholders; define wants and needs.	■ 3.1 Customer and Market Knowledge
■ Establish mission, vision, and values; define key business drivers; develop leadership processes to guide organization.	■ 1.1 Senior Leadership ■ 2.2 Strategy Development
■ Develop goals and strategies based on thorough analysis.	■ 2.1 Strategy Deployment ■ 2.2 Strategy Development
■ Identify key performance measures based on company strategy.	■ 3.2 Customer Relationships and Satisfaction ■ 4.1 Measurement, Analysis, and Improvement of Organizational Performance ■ 4.2 Management of Information, Information Technology, and Knowledge

What Successful Companies Do	Corresponding Baldrige Items
■ Review performance of all key measures, including financial, ethical, operational, supplier performance, customer satisfaction, and employee satisfaction.	■ 1.1 Senior Leadership ■ 7.1 Product and Service Outcomes ■ 7.2 Customer-Focused Outcomes ■ 7.3 Financial and Market Outcomes ■ 7.4 Workforce Outcomes ■ 7.5 Process Effectiveness Outcomes ■ 7.6 Leadership Outcomes
■ Design high quality products and/or services that meet current and future customer needs.	■ 6.1 Work System Design
■ Design jobs and organizations to promote high performance from employees; train and motivate employees to continuously delight customers.	■ 5.1 Workforce Engagement ■ 5.2 Workforce Environment
■ Define, control, and continuously improve key processes.	■ 6.2 Work Process Management and Improvement

What Successful Companies Do	Corresponding Baldrige Items
■ Work with suppliers and vendors to ensure consistent high-quality goods and services.	■ 6.2 Work Process Management and Improvement
■ Manage customer relationships to maintain high levels of satisfaction on an ongoing basis.	■ 3.2 Customer Relationships and Satisfaction
■ Exhibit good corporate citizenship; perform well in areas of public health, environment, and ethics.	■ 1.2 Governance and Social Responsibilities and Citizenship
■ Demonstrate excellent trends and levels in all results areas .	■ 7.1 Product and Service Outcomes ■ 7.2 Customer-Focused Outcomes ■ 7.3 Financial and Market Outcomes ■ 7.4 Workforce Outcomes ■ 7.5 Process Effectiveness Outcomes ■ 7.6 Leadership Outcomes

up to speed. This training can be supplemented with some packaged courses and training materials purchased from outside vendors.

A small organization also needs good financial, operational, and customer satisfaction results. Results are more crucial for a small organization because it may not have the reserves to survive a slow period or a loss of a major customer. All of the Baldrige criteria apply to a small organization, at least in spirit. Look for ways to meet the Baldrige ideals without adding too much formality to your systems and processes.

PART II
THE BALDRIGE
CRITERIA

A brief explanation of each of the 18 items in the Baldrige criteria and the characteristics of organizations that excel in each of these 18 factors.

1 Leadership (120 pts.)

Strong leadership and direction are keys to becoming a great organization. This first category asks how the senior leaders of an organization define its mission or purpose, the future vision, and the code of ethics or values by which the organization will be managed. The two items in Category 1 ask about the organization's leadership system (1.1 Senior Leadership) and how the organization leads in the areas of social responsibility and corporate citizenship (1.2 Governance and Social Responsibilities).

1.1 SENIOR LEADERSHIP: How do your senior leaders lead? (70 pts.)

Describe HOW SENIOR LEADERS guide and sustain your organization. Describe HOW SENIOR LEADERS communicate with your workforce and encourage HIGH PERFORMANCE.

What Does This Mean?

This item asks how clearly the senior executives have defined and communicated the mission of the organization, why it exists, its future direction, and the values for which it stands. Actions speak louder than words, so emphasis should be on how the behavior and decisions made by executives are in alignment with the mission, vision, and values. This item also asks about how the executives ensure honesty and ethical behavior using a system of governance. This system should protect the needs and interests of stockholders and other stakeholders. Finally, the item asks how the leaders review the performance of the organization to ensure that it is achieving its goals.

What Excellent Organizations Do

- Build a strong leadership team that is not dependent upon any one individual.

- Clearly communicate the mission, vision, and values, using plain language, not buzzwords.

- Ensure leaders behave and make decisions consistent with stated ethics and values.

- Create a strong culture and ensure that values endure as the organization grows and changes.

- Openly and honestly communicate with employees, customers, and other stakeholders.

- Continually look for future opportunities to improve the organization.

1.2 GOVERNANCE AND SOCIAL RESPONSIBILITIES: How do you govern and address your social responsibilities? (50 pts.)

Describe your organization's GOVERNANCE system. Describe HOW your organization addresses its responsibilities to the public, ensures ETHICAL BEHAVIOR, and practices good citizenship.

What Does This Mean?

This item asks for evidence that the company has a systematic approach to improve performance in public health and safety, environmental protection, and corporate citizenship. Companies should have goals for key aspects of performance in these areas, as well as plans to achieve the goals. The organization should be a leader and role model for other organizations.

It must also show leadership in corporate citizenship by supporting—and encouraging employee involvement in—schools, community groups, professional associations, and charities. Higher marks are given to organizations that are proactive in their approaches to corporate citizenship.

What Excellent Organizations Do

- Employ a thorough system of governance to make sure laws, rules, and values are consistently followed.

- Go beyond mandated performance levels in ethics, public safety, environmental, and other areas of regulation.

- Allocate significant resources for activities that relate to corporate citizenship and support of educational, community, charity, and professional organizations.

- Allow employees time on the job to support professional and community organizations.

- Link corporate citizenship efforts to marketing plans and organizational image.

2 Strategic Planning (85 pts.)

Category 2 asks how an organization pursues planning and what its plans are. Item 2.1 asks for a description of the planning process and a summary of the major objectives or goals. Item 2.2 asks about how plans are communicated, what action plans or initiatives will be used to achieve the goals or objectives, and for a forecast of where the organization will be if it achieves all its goals.

2.1 STRATEGY DEVELOPMENT: How do you develop your strategy? (40 pts.)

Describe HOW your organization determines its STRATEGIC CHALLENGES and advantages. Describe HOW your organization establishes its strategy and STRATEGIC OBJECTIVES to address these CHALLENGES and enhance its advantages. Summarize your organization's KEY STRATEGIC OBJECTIVES and their related GOALS.

What Does This Mean?

This item asks two basic questions: how you pursue planning and what are your major goals or objectives? This item builds on the mission, vision,

22

and values defined in the leadership category, and asks how the organization addresses the challenges and threats it faces and how it plans to capitalize on its current strengths. It is important that a variety of internal and external factors are considered during planning. It is also important that planning is accomplished quickly and efficiently. Plans often change, so it should be simple to make adjustments when necessary. Goals and objectives should be well balanced, addressing all areas of performance, including financial outcomes and measures of customers, markets, products and services, and workforce.

What Excellent Organizations Do

- Complete a thorough situation analysis that looks at strengths, weaknesses, opportunities, and threats, using a systematic model like Baldrige.

- Write annual and longer-term strategic plans in 1 to 2 months with minimal drafts.

- Focus the planning process on strategic thinking rather than creating a binder.

- Develop clear and thoughtful goals or objectives, linked to the vision and situation analysis, along with additional challenges the organization will face.

- Develop plans that address all aspects of performance—not only financial aspects.

2.2 STRATEGY DEPLOYMENT: How do you deploy your strategy? (45 pts.)

Describe HOW your organization converts its STRATEGIC OBJECTIVES into ACTION PLANS. Summarize your organization's ACTION PLANS and related KEY PERFORMANCE MEASURES or INDICATORS. Project your organization's future PERFORMANCE on these KEY PERFORMANCE MEASURES or INDICATORS.

What Does This Mean?

This item asks about how you develop specific measures and targets, and the strategies that will be used to achieve those targets. Annual and longer-term targets should be specified for each performance measure. In addition, you must present a summary of the initiatives or action plans that will be used to accomplish your goals and targets. This item also asks about where you will be in the next 3 to 5 years relative to key competitors and benchmark organizations if you hit all your targets.

What Excellent Organizations Do

- Identify key success factors that differentiate your organization from key competitors.

- Set measurable targets for each measure of performance based upon relevant data (e.g., competitors, resources, customer needs, etc.).

- Define specific strategies or action plans for hitting targets.

- Communicate plans to all levels of employees and partners so they understand their roles in helping the organization achieve its vision.

- Adapt or change targets and strategies quickly as the business environment changes.

- Predict how achievement of targets will change the organization's position in the marketplace over the next 2 to 5 years.

3 Customer and Market Focus (85 pts.)

This category asks you to identify customers and their requirements and manage relationships that keep them satisfied. Item 3.1 asks how you identify customers and define their needs. Item 3.2 asks how you win and keep customers and addresses customer satisfaction measures.

3.1 CUSTOMER AND MARKET KNOWLEDGE: How do you use customer and market knowledge? (40 pts.)

*Describe **HOW** your organization determines requirements, needs, expectations, and preferences of **CUSTOMERS** and markets to ensure the continuing relevance of your products and services and develop new business opportunities.*

What Does This Mean?

This is the first item in the systems model of the criteria shown on the inside cover. It relates to identifying your target markets and customers and what they want and expect from your products and/or services. You might list the targeted groups or market segments, and identify their individual priorities. It is also important to explain how you determine customer requirements and expectations. It is important not only to use several methods to identify customer requirements, but to use them often. Customers' wants and expectations change frequently.

This item also asks about future customers, and what their requirements will be. These are difficult questions to answer; however, the most successful companies today look at industry trends and predict how they will impact their products and/or services. Successful companies also look beyond current customers and identify new industries or types of customers.

As with all Baldrige items that question approaches, it is important to show a trend of continuously evaluating and improving methods of identifying customer requirements.

What Excellent Organizations Do

- Clearly identify customers and segment them by market, geography, or other categories.

- Use a variety of methods to identify customer requirements and priorities.

- Continuously evaluate and improve methods to determine customer requirements.

- Conduct research to identify potential future markets or customers and their needs.

- Identify the requirements of potential customers and customers of competitors.

3.2 CUSTOMER RELATIONSHIPS AND SATISFACTION: How do you build relationships and grow customer satisfaction and loyalty? (45 pts.)

Describe HOW your organization builds relationships to acquire, satisfy, and retain CUSTOMERS and to increase CUSTOMER loyalty. Describe also HOW your organization determines CUSTOMER satisfaction and dissatisfaction.

What Does This Mean?

This item concerns keeping customers happy after you have won their business. Most organizations spend more money to gain customers than they do to retain customers. This section asks for evidence of a proactive approach to keeping customers satisfied on an ongoing basis.

Another dimension of keeping customers satisfied is providing an easy outlet for them to seek information and report complaints. Have a system for tracking all complaints and promptly resolve complaints when they occur. When customers complain, they present you with an opportunity to win back their trust and good will.

Item 3.1 asks how you learn about customer requirements. It also relates to how you measure what customers think of your products and/or services after they are purchased.

You should have hard and soft measures of customer satisfaction. Hard measures relate to measures of customer buying behavior. Soft measures are opinions gathered through surveys, interviews, and focus groups.

Along with a good mix of hard and soft customer satisfaction data, it is much better to tailor measurements to your own markets or customer types rather than using a generic customer satisfaction survey. Finally, it is important to describe how you build loyalty from important customers, taking into account that customer needs and priorities vary.

What Excellent Organizations Do

- Hire the best and brightest customer contact people, pay them well, train them thoroughly,

29

and give them the authority to solve customer problems without checking with management.

- Define measurable service standards and measure performance against them.

- Provide toll-free help lines or conveniences to make it easy for customers to get information.

- Track all complaints, no matter how minor and resolve them quickly.

- Accumulate information on customers in a central database so that this intelligence can be used to drive improvement.

- Collect a good mix of hard and soft measures of customer satisfaction.

- Define customer satisfaction levels compared to key competitor and industry averages.

- Focus on measuring value and loyalty as well as customer satisfaction.

- Employ a systematic approach to building loyalty from the most valued customers.

4 Measurement, Analysis, and Knowledge Management (90 pts.)

Category 4 is a core part of the Baldrige criteria that asks how you measure the performance of the organization and how you analyze performance data to make decisions. Item 4.1 asks you to identify the set of metrics you track—many organizations refer to this information as a scorecard. Item 4.1 also asks how the measures link back to goals and other important factors for overall success. Item 4.2 asks about the use of information technology and how you manage organizational knowledge.

4.1 MEASUREMENT, ANALYSIS, AND IMPROVEMENT OF ORGANIZATIONAL PERFORMANCE: How do you measure, analyze, and review organizational performance? (45 pts.)

Describe HOW your organization measures, analyzes, aligns, and improves its PERFORMANCE data and information at all LEVELS and in all parts of your organization. Describe HOW you SYSTEMATICALLY use the results of your reviews to evaluate and improve PROCESSES.

What Does This Mean?

This item asks about the high-level performance metrics that are collected to evaluate organizational performance on a regular basis. Metrics should include financial, customer, employee, and other categories of measures that address your various stakeholders. Measures should be balanced to include long- and short-term indicators, metrics that relate to your mission or ongoing business, and those that are more strategic and relate to your vision.

This item also asks about how you analyze performance based on these various measures to set targets and make decisions about commitment of resources and development of strategies. Forward-thinking organizations have identified correlations between measures such as employee and customer loyalty and financial performance. Understanding the links among the various measures in your corporate dashboard is vitally important in achieving overall goals. Communicating this information to appropriate personnel is also assessed.

What Excellent Organizations Do

- Develop measures linked to the vision or strategy and the overall mission of the organization.

- Keep the number of metrics that any manager or executive reviews to no more than 20.

- Include a balance of measures that focus on the past, present, and future, and relate the information to the needs of shareholders or owners, customers, and employees.

- Collect a wide variety of data about key competitors and comparative organizations.

- Conduct research to identify links or correlations between leading and lagging metrics on the company dashboard.

- Spend as much time focusing on measures that lead to future success as on metrics that depict past and present performance.

4.2 MANAGEMENT OF INFORMATION, INFORMATION TECHNOLOGY, AND KNOWLEDGE: How do you manage your information, information technology, and organizational knowledge? (45 pts.)

Describe HOW your organization ensures the quality and availability of needed data, information, software, and hardware for your WORKFORCE, suppliers, PARTNERS, COLLABORATORS, and CUSTOMERS . Describe HOW your organization builds and manages its KNOWLEDGE ASSETS.

What Does This Mean?

This item asks how you use information technology to provide leaders and other members of the workforce with the data, tools, and resources they need to perform their jobs. In a large organization this might consist of the latest computer software and hardware. In a smaller organization, communication may be less dependent on technology, but is still important to use the best technology that the organization can afford. Communication of performance information in spreadsheets with endless columns of hard-to-read numbers is far from an ideal approach.

The collective knowledge of the workforce in most of today's organizations is far more valuable than any physical assets. Criteria item 4.2 also asks how you manage and document this knowledge so that it may be transferred to others. Building a knowledge data base or implementing a knowledge management program is only part of the answer. Having access to people who have the knowledge and skills needed is far more effective than pulling information from a data base.

What Excellent Organizations Do

- Communicate up-to-date performance data using consistent graphics and formats across the organization.

- Use the best custom-designed or packaged scorecard software on the market to communicate performance data.

- Make use of organization intranet sites and other appropriate methods to communicate real-time performance data to all necessary personnel.

- Standardize data collection and reporting methods to ensure consistency and data integrity.

- Regularly evaluate and improve software and hardware used for data collection, reporting, and analysis.

- Have a system for documenting knowledge and best practices that is easily accessible by all who may use it.

5 Workforce Focus (85 pts.)

Category 5 asks how you build a strong workforce, slot people in the right jobs, train them, and keep them motivated or engaged so they consistently achieve high performance. The two items in this category ask about workforce engagement (5.1) and the workforce environment (5.2).

5.1 WORKFORCE ENGAGEMENT: How do you engage your workforce to achieve organizational and personal success? (45 pts.)

Describe HOW your organization engages, compensates, and rewards HIGH PERFORMANCE. Describe HOW members of your WORKFORCE, including leaders, are developed to achieve HIGH PERFORMANCE. Describe how you assess your WORKFORCE ENGAGEMENT and use the results to achieve higher PERFORMANCE.

What Does This Mean?

This item asks about designing a culture that promotes high performance from all members of your workforce. Factors addressed include communication, goal setting, and feedback. This item also asks how you determine what motivates different categories and types of employees and leaders. The second factor this item assesses is how you develop and train your workforce. It is important to link training and development to overall organizational goals and strategies. Finally, this item asks how you measure levels of workforce engagement or satisfaction and how data on these metrics are used to drive improvement efforts.

What Excellent Organizations Do

- Identify the most important factors that motivate various categories and types of employees.

- Design reward systems and jobs to encourage high performance and engagement from all members of the workforce.

- Invest up to 5% of payroll costs on workforce training and development each year.

- Conduct systematic needs analyses to identify knowledge and skill gaps and link these analyses to strategic plans.

- Design and implement efficient and objective systems for frequent workforce feedback and performance management that go far beyond a typical annual appraisal.

5.2 WORKFORCE ENVIRONMENT: How do you build an effective and supportive workforce environment? (40 pts.)

Describe HOW your organization manages WORKFORCE CAPABILITY and CAPACITY to accomplish the work of the organization. Describe HOW your organization maintains a safe, secure, and supportive work climate.

What Does This Mean?

This item asks how you determine the knowledge, skills, and values of your current and future workforces and how you find people to fill those needs. It also asks how you place new and existing employees into jobs where they are most likely to excel and how you prepare people for changes in the nature of your business. Item 5.2 also asks about workforce safety, security, and health. These factors exert huge impacts on workforce performance and costs in today's organizations. Finally, this item asks about workforce benefits, services, and other factors designed to create positive work environments.

What Excellent Organizations Do

- Design jobs and organizational structures to promote communication, cooperation, innovation, and behavior consistent with the values and culture of the organization.

- Thoroughly screen potential new hires and candidates for promotion for appropriate knowledge, skills, and values.

- Tailor human resources systems and practices to the culture and mission of the organization rather than implementing each new management fad that comes along.

- Implement a prevention-based approach to workforce health, safety, and security.

- Monitor preventive and lagging measures of workforce health, safety, and security on a regular basis and install a systematic approach for implementing action plans when data shows declines in performance.

- Provide an innovative array of benefits and services for employees designed to foster their loyalty and reduce stress.

6 Process Management (85 pts.)

This important category of the criteria asks about completing work, managing control, and improving major work processes. The category breaks down into two items. Both ask about "work systems" that constitute a collection of processes that may be performed within or outside the organization. For example, selling cars is a process in a car company work system that is performed by independent dealers. Item 6.1 covers work system design and seeks information on how your organization designs its major processes and decides which processes will be performed internally or externally. Item 6.2 asks how work processes are controlled and improved.

6.1 WORK SYSTEMS DESIGN: How do you design your work systems? (45 pts.)

Describe HOW your organization determines its CORE COMPETENCIES and designs its WORK SYSTEMS and KEY PROCESSES to deliver CUSTOMER VALUE, prepare for potential emergencies, and achieve organizational success and SUSTAINABILITY.

What Does This Mean?

The first question relates to your "core competencies" or areas of greatest expertise—areas in which the organization excels and results that competitors will find difficult to copy. For example, a core competency of a company like Bose is innovative product design. A core competency of a school may be science education. The next question concerns the most important requirements are for each of your key work processes, and how these requirements were determined. It is critical to link requirements and standards back to research on customer requirements and process variables that link to important outcomes. Finally, this item asks how your organization prepares for various types of disasters that might cause devastation if plans are not in place.

What Excellent Organizations Do

- Honestly identify their own strengths or core competencies and farm out other processes or work to suppliers or partners.

- Incorporate the best practices of benchmark organizations when designing work system sand processes.

- Identify the key requirements for each major work process through research and analysis of customer requirements, and process constraints.

- Design work processes to minimize cycle time—get things done as quickly and efficiently as possible.

- Implement a prevention-based approach to planning for various types of emergencies and disasters.

6.2 WORK PROCESS MANAGEMENT AND IMPROVEMENT: How do you manage and improve your key organizational work processes? (50 pts.)

Describe HOW your organization implements, manages, and improves its KEY work PROCESSES to deliver CUSTOMER VALUE and achieve organizational success and SUSTAINABILITY.

What Does This Mean?

This item asks how you manage and control your key work processes. What is important for many processes in an organization is consistency. McDonalds, for example, carefully controls all of its processes to ensure that customers get the same product from every restaurant. For other processes that involve creativity, such as teaching cursive to third graders, consistency is not as important as a process measure. What is important for all processes is that they are properly documented and measured, and that measures and/or standards link back to important measures of outcomes. This item also asks how your organization evaluates and improves its processes. Trying to improve all process is an expensive waste of time. Rather, process improvements should be systematic and very selective. The processes chosen for improvement should be those that are defective—their improvement will make a significant impact on the organization's goals.

What Excellent Organizations Do

- Define and document the key work processes involved in producing the organization's products and/or services.

- Define and track process measures that link back to important outcome measures.

- Implement control strategies to ensure that standards are consistently met or exceeded.

- Avoid over-engineering or controlling process that call for innovation and creativity.

- Focus on reducing cycle time for all key processes.

- Link process improvement efforts to performance data and strategic plans.

- Consider many sources of ideas for improving work processes, including looking outside the organization and its industry.

7 Results (450 pts.)

Category 7 is the final and most important of the categories and is worth almost half of the total points in a Baldrige assessment (450 of 1000). It covers all the important results that an organization tracks—a total of six items: Section: 7.1, Product and Service Outcomes; Section 7.2, Customer-Focused Outcomes; Section 7.3, Financial and Market Outcomes; Section 7.4, Workforce-Focused Outcomes; Section 7.5, Process Effectiveness Outcomes; and Section 7.6, Leadership Outcomes. An organization is expected to show excellent levels of performance compared to other organizations and trends that show stable or improving performance over multiple years in all six areas.

7.1 PRODUCT AND SERVICE OUTCOMES: What are your product service performance results? (100 pts.)

Summarize your organization's KEY product and service PERFORMANCE RESULTS. SEGMENT your RESULTS by product and service types and groups, CUSTOMER groups, and market SEGMENTS, as appropriate. Include appropriate comparative data.

What Does This Mean?

This important first item asks for data on factors such as quality, timeliness, and other important metrics that link back to customer requirements. An airline might report on-time landings; a hospital would detail clinical outcome measures; a school might report student test scores; and a business might report defects found in products. This section is worth slightly more points than the other five in Category 7 because it addresses the major reasons for an organization to exist. Trends should be shown for spans of 5 or more years; all measures should show comparisons of your organization's performance to competitor, benchmark, and other relevant data.

Results in Excellent Organizations

- Key measures of product or service performance show an improving trend over 5 or more years or a consistently high level of performance.

- Comparative data show that your product or service performance is better than performance of major competitors and much better than averages in your industry.

- Results in these areas link back to important customer requirements and standards.

- No graphs of product or service performance show declining performance trends or levels below industry averages.

- Occasional dips in performance have been analyzed and corrected.

- Clear links can be seen between process measures and standards identified in Section 6.1 and the outcome or output measures shown here.

7.2 CUSTOMER-FOCUSED OUTCOMES: What are your customer-focused performance results? (70 pts.)

Summarize your organization's KEY CUSTOMER-focused RESULTS, including CUSTOMER satisfaction and CUSTOMER-perceived VALUE. Segment your RESULTS by product and service types and groups, CUSTOMER groups, and market SEGMENTS, as appropriate. Include appropriate comparative data.

What Does This Mean?

This item asks for graphs and performance data relating to customer satisfaction with your products or services over the past few years. Measures typically reported in this section include soft measures of customer opinions gathered via surveys, interviews, focus groups, and even complaints. It is also appropriate to include hard measures of customer behavior such as repeat business, referrals, loyalty, increases in your business, and decreases in competitor businesses. Measures of customer dissatisfaction should also be presented. To evaluate levels and trends in performance, all graphs should include relevant competitor and comparative data.

Results in Excellent Organizations

- Customer satisfaction data are segmented by market or customer type as appropriate, and all graphs show excellent improvement trends.

- No graphs of customer-focused results show flat or declining performance; all dips in performance are satisfactorily explained.

- All major indicators of customer dissatisfaction show declines over the past 5 or more years and overall excellent levels of performance.

- Trends over the past 3 or more years show continuous improvement in hard measures of customer satisfaction and internal quality measures.

- Levels of performance on hard measures of customer satisfaction show the best performance in the industry on most graphs and benchmark or world-class levels of performance on several graphs.

7.3 FINANCIAL AND MARKET OUTCOMES: What are your financial and marketplace results? (70 pts.)

Summarize your organization's KEY financial and marketplace PERFORMANCE RESULTS by

CUSTOMER or market SEGMENTS, as appropriate. Include appropriate comparative data.

What Does This Mean?

This item asks for two types of results or data: market and financial results. Market results may include gains and losses of customers or shares of certain markets. Financial results are the typical financial measures companies collect data on such as sales, profits, and return on investment. All key market and financial measures should be identified in Item 4.1. You should have graphs of results on each of these measures for 5 years or more. As with the previous item, results in this area are evaluated by analyzing levels, trends, and variabilities.

Results in Excellent Organizations

- Key financial and market results for 5 or more years show a trend of progressive improvement.

- Profits show a level of performance comparable to or better than the best organizations in the industry.

- Clear cause-and-effect data show that investments in improvement initiatives have paid off on the bottom line.

49

- Market and financial measures show benchmark levels of performance or at least a continuously improving trend spanning 5 or more years.

- No graphs of market or financial indicators show performance to be flat or worsening over the past few years.

- Dips in performance have been thoroughly analyzed and the factors causing these drops in performance have been corrected.

7.4 WORKFORCE-FOCUSED OUTCOMES: What are your workforce-focused performance results? (70 pts.)

Summarize your organization's KEY WORKFORCE-focused RESULTS for WORKFORCE ENGAGEMENT and for your WORKFORCE environment. SEGMENT your RESULTS to address the DIVERSITY of your WORKFORCE and to address your WORKFORCE groups and SEGMENTS, as appropriate. Include appropriate comparative data.

What Does This Mean?

This item asks for levels and trends in key human resource measures such as safety, turnover, employee engagement, and absenteeism.

This category might also include other measures identified in Category 5, for example, training effectiveness measures or percentages of employee suggestions implemented. Other statistics concerning employee recognition and compensation measures might also be presented.

Comparative data on how human resource performance compares with competitors, industry averages, and benchmarks should also be presented to aid in evaluating levels of performance.

Results in Excellent Organizations

- Safety results show that impressive improvement trends and/or levels of performance are superior to industry averages and competitors.

- Measures of employee satisfaction and engagement show excellent levels and trends.

- Hard measures of employee dissatisfaction such as absenteeism and voluntary turnover show improving trends and levels above those of competitors.

- No workforce performance measures show declining trends or levels inferior to industry averages or major competitors.

- Results are presented for all key human resource measures identified in Category 5.

7.5 PROCESS EFFECTIVENESS OUTCOMES: What are your process effectiveness results? (70 pts.)

Summarize your organization's KEY operational PERFORMANCE RESULTS that contribute to the improvement of organizational EFFECTIVENESS, including your organization's readiness for emergencies. SEGMENT your RESULTS by product and service types and groups, by PROCESSES and location, and by market SEGMENTS, as appropriate. Include appropriate comparative data.

What Does This Mean?

This tends to be a large item in the Baldrige Award application because it includes graphs of many measures of performance. Typical measures reported in Item 7.5 include productivity, efficiency, cycle time, schedule performance, production measures, and measures of supplier and partner performance. Each industry also tends to have its own unique metrics to report for this item. For example, an airline might report maintenance cost per mile flown and a hotel might report revenue per available room. As with other items in Category 7, make sure that appropriate competitor and comparative data are included on all graphs.

Results in Excellent Organizations

- Results are presented for all key performance measures for which results are not presented earlier.

- Productivity and cycle time both show impressive levels and improvement trends.

- Data on important process measures show improvements and high levels.

- Most graphs should show company performance to be better than performances of most of all key competitors.

- No data are missing on important measures of operational performance.

- Strong improvement trends in the performance of the organization's major suppliers and partners are evident over the past few years.

- Levels of performance compare favorably to those of competitors' and benchmark organizations' suppliers.

7.6 LEADERSHIP OUTCOMES: What are your leadership results? (70 pts.)

Summarize your organization's KEY GOVERNANCE and SENIOR LEADERSHIP RESULTS, including evidence of strategic plan accomplishments, ETHICAL BEHAVIOR, fiscal accountability, legal compliance, social responsibility, and organizational citizenship. SEGMENT your RESULTS by organizational units, as appropriate. Include appropriate comparative data.

What Does This Mean?

This final item asks for results that show your organization behaves in an ethical and socially responsible manner. It also asks for evidence that shows progress toward your vision and strategic goals. Many of the measures reported here should have been identified in Sections 1.1 and 1.2. Five types of results are sought: (1) strategic measures linked to vision, goals, and strategies for meeting key challenges or targets; (2) performance on measures of ethical behavior such as increases in dismissals or disciplinary actions for unethical actions, employee opinions on real organizational ethics, and increased use of screening techniques for hiring and promotion; (3) measures of fiscal responsibility that might include measures of risk stock performance, links between company performance and executive compensation and penalties, and increasing trends in thoroughness and frequency of financial audits; (4) measures showing compliance with legal and regulatory requirements; (5) measures demonstrating support of charities and other community organizations. As with all result areas, it is important to show trends over multiple years, targets, and comparative data to prove that your organization is not typical and is a top performer in your industry and community.

Results in Excellent Organizations

- Results presented show clear progress toward vision and strategic goals.

- Results are presented for all key performance measures identified in Item 1.2 or elsewhere in the application.

- Clear improvement trends can be seen in the organization's level of fiscal responsibility.

- Results show excellent levels and trends in meaningful measures of ethical behavior and stakeholder trust.

- External data indicate a high level of respect for the organization's ethics and fiscal responsibility.

- No negative trends or results can be found in the areas of legal and/or regulatory compliance.

- Results show that the organization is a leader in its support of community and charitable groups.

For Additional Reading

Brown, Mark Graham. *Baldrige Award Winning Quality*, 16th Edition. New York: Productivity Press, 2008.

Brown, Mark Graham. *Get It, Set It, Move It, Prove It: 60 Ways to Get Real Results in Your Organization*. New York: Productivity Press, 2004.

Garvin, David. "How the Baldrige Award Really Works," *Harvard Business Review*, November/December, 1991, p. 80–95.

Hart, Christopher W.L. and Christopher Bogan. *The Baldrige: What It Is, How It's Won, How to Use It to Improve Quality in Your Company*, New York: McGraw-Hill Inc., 1992.

Hutton, David W. *From Baldrige to the Bottom Line: A Roadmap for Organizational Change and Improvement*, Milwaukee: American Society for Quality, 2000.

National Institute of Standards and Technology, *2007 Criteria for Performance Excellence*, Gaithersburg, MD: NIST, 2007.

ABOUT THE AUTHOR

Mark Graham Brown has conducted training and provided consulting on the application of the Baldrige principles since 1990. He has worked with corporate and government clients in the U.S. and 15 other countries. Additional information on his services and other books can be found on his web site: markgrahambrown. com.